RENAISSANCE

Boris von Brauchitsch

BARRON'S

First edition for the United States and Canada published by
Barron's Educational Series, Inc., 2000.

First published in Germany in 1999 by DuMont Buchverlag GmbH und Co.
Kommanditgesellschaft, Köln, Germany

English text version by: Agents - Producers - Editors, Overath, Germany
Translated by: Sally Schreiber, Cologne, Germany
Edited by: Bessie Blum, Cambridge, MA

All inquiries should be addressed to:
Barron's Educational Series, Inc.
250 Wireless Boulevard
Hauppauge, New York 11788
http://www.barronseduc.com

International Standard Book No. 0-7641-1336-4

Library of Congress Catalog Card No. 99-65090

Printed in Italy
987654321